Sam
Sees All

AIREDALE JUNIOR SCHOOL
FRYSTON ROAD
AIREDALE
CASTLEFORD
WF10 3EP

Miss Plum is sad. Things at the zoo keep going missing.

I have lost my ring.

The big cats have lost their keeper. Some animals are missing too.

Miss Plum needs Sam to help.
Sam can help to see lost things.

I can see right into things.

Sam sees all!

Sam looks for the keeper.

He looks right into a big cat.

He sees the keeper asleep!

Sam rubs the big cat ...

... out comes the keeper!

Sam looks for the missing animals.

Zoo

Freezer Phil

He spots Freezer Phil pinching them!

6

Sam must get the animals back.

Siss will help you get the animals back.

Siss

Sam and Siss go to Freezer Phil's den.

They spot all the missing animals.

Freezer Phil has been freezing their zoo!

Sam and Siss must get the Frost Zapper.

With one whoosh, Siss grabs the Frost Zapper.

Whoosh!

Go for it, Siss!

It is off to jail for Freezer Phil.
Oh! Jail is no fun!
Nee nar!
Whizz!
Nee nar!

Sam returns the animals to the zoo.
He thinks all is well, but ...

Sam looks for the little ring.

The ring is in Siss!

Miss Plum will get the ring back soon.